This
Home Owner's Journal
Belongs To:

Name _____

Address _____

City, State, ZIP _____

Phone _____

QUICK REFERENCE PHONE NUMBERS

TYPE OF WORK	NAME	PHONE
Air Conditioner		
Carpenter		
Carpet Cleaner		
Drapery Cleaner		
Electrician		
General Handyperson		
Heating		
Lawn Maintenance		
Home Insurance		
Painter		
Paperer		
Plumber		
Sewer/Cesspool/Septic		
Other		

The Home Owner's Journal:

What I Did and When I Did It

By Colleen Jenkins

Third Edition

BLUE SKY MARKETING, INC.
P.O. Box 21583-S St. Paul, MN 55121

The Home Owner's Journal:
What I Did and When I Did It

By Colleen Jenkins

Third Edition

Potsy Series: Book One

Copyright (c) 1991, 1988, and 1987 by Colleen Jenkins

Cover Design by Julia Schreifels

Printed in the United States of America

Published by:

BLUE SKY MARKETING, INC.
P.O. Box 21583-S
St. Paul, MN 55121
(612) 456-5602
SAN 263-9394

ISBN 0-911493-11-5

20   19   18   17   16   15   14   13

TABLE OF CONTENTS

TABLE OF CONTENTS (continued)

IMPORTANT NOTICE

This book contains general guidelines on what information you may want to keep for annual income tax and capital gain tax reporting purposes. The tax information was provided by one of the world's largest and most respected accounting firms, Ernst & Whinney. Many specific examples are given. The list, however, is not exhaustive, and as is always the case with tax laws, there are many items that may vary on a state-by-state and case-by-case basis. If you have any questions, check with a competent tax professional.

The author and publisher are not dispensing accounting, legal, or other professional advice. Seek the advice of a competent tax, legal, or other professional if you need help.

THANK YOU!!

At the request of the publisher, we both kept a running list of every person who has contributed to this book. When the book was finally ready for press and we looked over the list, I was amazed that more than ninety people contributed! A big THANK YOU to all of you!

A special thanks to Thomas Dougherty, CPA, Attorney at Law, who provided us with some excellent tax material.

IMPORTANT PERSONAL PAPERS

List your important personal papers and where they are kept. Examples are your Will, life insurance policies, fire insurance policies, stocks and bonds. Also list the location of your safe deposit box and all bank accounts. Include policy limits and the name of your attorney, agents, and brokers, etc. Tell your emergency contact person(s) about this book and where it can be found.

Item   **Details**

_____

_____

_____

_____

_____

_____

_____

_____

_____

_____

_____

_____

_____

_____

_____

_____

_____

_____

_____

HOW TO USE YOUR JOURNAL

This is the book I have needed. I don't know how I managed without it. The fact is, I did not manage well at all. In the years that I have owned my home, I finally made the same type of mistake one too many times and decided to find a solution. I don't recall the precise instant, but it was either when I recently wallpapered the bathroom or when I painted the outside of the house.

The consequence of my failure to write down how much paint I used the last time was two gallons of custom mixed, non-returnable paint left over *after* I *finished* painting the house. Had I written down the amount I used the previous time, I would have saved myself over $20!

When I estimated how often things like that probably happened in the more than thirty years I have lived in my home, the need for this book became painfully clear. Believe me, I do NOT have money or time to waste.

I thought this book would be simple to do, but I actually wrote many drafts before arriving at what I think is a very practical, easy-to-use, and flexible journal. No two homes are identical, so complete only the sections that are applicable to your home. (Don't forget to change the Table of Contents, too!)

If your book is neat and unmarked, it means you aren't using it to its full potential. Fill it out. Give it a work-out and you'll be rewarded with all the information you will ever want and need -- all in one, well-organized book.

Immediately following this introduction are two pages for recording purchase, finance, and insurance information. After that, there are six main chapters: Interior, Exterior, Cooling & Heating, Insulation, Miscellaneous, and Getting Organized. The sections within each chapter are organized in alphabetical order, except where items have special relationships to each other.

Most main sections contain an additional page for extra notes. The note pages can also be used as graph paper for drawings, etc. You may want to sketch the walls with windows and door measurements, wiring projects, or make notes about what you may want to consider next time.

In order to offer as much flexibility as possible, some sections are comprised of only a heading and lined paper for writing or drawing. This will enable you to tailor the section to fit your particular needs.

You will probably save yourself some frustration if you make all entries in pencil. This will allow you to easily make corrections and updates.

Finally, the Getting Organized chapter wraps the book up with sections explaining what records to keep for tax purposes; instructions for setting up an easy-to-use filing system for important receipts, warranties, and other papers; and information on some other products to help you and your friends get organized.

An example of how a portion of a page might look when filled out follows.

Good luck! Let me know what you think of the book & how we can improve it. Suggestions from readers were incorporated into this edition. Maybe yours will be in the next!

SAMPLE ROOM NUMBER 1

CEILING COVERING

Type of Covering (paint, spray texture, etc.) *Paint*

Purchased From *Swan Hardware* Date *2/2/87*

Brand & Pattern *Ripple Paints*

Color & No. *Silver Smoke* #*94317* Warranty Period _____

Applied with (texture roller, sprayer, etc.) *Brush and Roller*

Cost/Unit $*8.88* No. of Units *2 gal.* Total $*17.76*

Installed By *Colleen*

Date *2-8-87* Cost $_____

Notes: *Only needed one gallon and one quart*

PURCHASE, FINANCE, & INSURANCE

PURCHASE INFORMATION

Date You Moved In _____

Property Legal Description (block, lot no., etc.) _____

Builder/Contractor's Company _____

    Contact Person _____

      Phone No. _____

    Date Home Built (completed) _____

    Warrantee on Construction _____

Land Development Company _____

    Contact Person _____

      Phone No. _____

Real Estate Company _____

    Agent _____

      Work Phone No. _____ Home Phone No. _____

Notes: _____

_____

FINANCE INFORMATION

Mortgage Company _____

    Loan Officer _____

      Work Phone No. _____ Home Phone No. _____

    Loan No. _____

      Loan Servicing Dept. Phone No. _____

New Mortgage Company (if your mortgage is sold) _____

    Phone No. _____

    Loan No. _____

    Date Sold _____

    Mortgage Balance at Time of Sale _____

Notes: _____

_____

Second Mortgage Company _____

    Phone No. _____

    Loan No. _____

    Date _____

    Balance of Principal on Original _____

Mortgage Information

    Purchase Price _____ Price Asked _____

    Downpayment _____ Appraised Value _____

    Mortgage Amount _____ Location of Abstract _____

    Mortgage Type (FHA, VA, Conventional, etc.) _____

    Interest Rate (beginning, if adjustable*) _____

    Terms (30 yr. fixed, adjustable*, etc.) _____

    Points (no. & $ amount) _____

    Realtor's Commission (% & $) _____

    Other Closing Costs _____

    Closing Date _____

*Adjustable Rate Mortgage (ARM) Information

Rate	Date of Change	Principal Remaining	Monthly P & I

Adjustment Interval _____

Index _____

Margin _____

Interest Rate Caps (yearly, lifetime, etc.) _____

_____

Monthly Payment Cap _____

Graduated Payments _____

Negative Amortization (y/n & limit) _____

"Introductory" Rate _____

Assumability _____

Convertibility _____

Prepayment Privilege _____

Points (including origination fee) _____

INSURANCE INFORMATION

Title Insurance Company _____

Title Binder No. _____

Homeowner's Insurance Company _____

Agent's Name _____

Work Phone No. _____ Home Phone No. _____

Policy No. _____

Expiration Date (if pre-paid) _____

Extra Notes: _____

_____

_____

_____

_____

_____

_____

_____

_____

ATTIC

(Use tick marks at top & bottom to make graph paper)

BASEMENT

(Use tick marks at top & bottom to make graph paper)

BATHROOM NUMBER 1
FLOOR COVERING

Floor Measurements

Widest part of room from middle of doorway _____

Longest part of room from middle of doorway _____

Notes: _____

Type of Covering (carpet, tile, etc.) _____

Purchased From _____ Date _____

Brand & Pattern _____

Color & No. _____ Warranty Period _____

Type of Backing _____ Pad Type _____

Cost/Unit $_____ No. of Units _____ Total $_____

Installed By _____ Attached With _____

Date _____ Cost $_____

Cleaned/Refinished By _____

Date 1 _____ Cost $_____

Date 2 _____ Cost $_____

Notes: _____

_____

CEILING COVERING

Type of Covering (paint, spray texture, etc.) _____

Purchased From _____ Date _____

Brand & Pattern _____

Color & No. _____ Warranty Period _____

Applied with (texture roller, sprayer, etc.) _____

Cost/Unit $_____ No. of Units _____ Total $_____

Installed By _____

Date _____ Cost $_____

Notes: _____

_____

WINDOW COVERING

Window 1 Measurements

Height _____ Width _____ Top of Window to Floor _____

Type of Covering (draperies, blinds, etc.) _____

Purchased From _____ Cost $_____ Date _____

　　Measurements of Window Covering _____

　　Fabric & Cleaning Instructions _____

Cleaned By _____ Cost $_____ Date _____

Notes: _____

Window 2 Measurements

Height _____ Width _____ Top of Window to Floor _____

Type of Covering (draperies, blinds, etc.) _____

Purchased From _____ Cost $_____ Date _____

　　Measurements of Window Covering _____

　　Fabric & Cleaning Instructions _____

Cleaned By _____ Cost $_____ Date _____

Notes: _____

WALL COVERING

Wall Measurements

North _____ South _____ East _____ West _____

Note: Use "2nd Type of Covering" for woodwork or panelling. It has a "Refinished By" section.

1st Type of Covering (paint, paper, etc.) _____

Purchased From _____ Date _____

　　Brand & Pattern _____

　　Color & No. _____ Warranty Period _____

　　Cost/Unit $_____ No. of Units _____ Total $_____

Installed By _____

　　Date _____ Cost $_____

Notes: _____

WALL COVERING (continued)

2nd Type of Covering (woodwork, panelling, etc.) _____

Purchased From _____ Date _____

   Brand & Pattern _____

   Color & No. _____ Warranty Period _____

   Cost/Unit $_____ No. of Units _____ Total $_____

Installed By _____

   Date _____ Cost $_____

Refinished By _____

   Date _____ Cost $_____

Notes: _____

SAMPLES: PAINT, WALLPAPER, ETC.

attach swatch or paint daub here

FURNITURE/APPLIANCES

Item	Purchased From	Date	Cost	Warranty

EXTRA NOTES

(Use tick marks at top & bottom to make graph paper)

BATHROOM NUMBER 2

FLOOR COVERING

Floor Measurements

Widest part of room from middle of doorway _____

Longest part of room from middle of doorway _____

Notes: _____

Type of Covering (carpet, tile, etc.) _____

Purchased From _____ Date _____

Brand & Pattern _____

Color & No. _____ Warranty Period _____

Type of Backing _____ Pad Type _____

Cost/Unit $_____ No. of Units _____ Total $_____

Installed By _____ Attached With _____

Date _____ Cost $_____

Cleaned/Refinished By _____

Date 1 _____ Cost $_____

Date 2 _____ Cost $_____

Notes: _____

_____

CEILING COVERING

Type of Covering (paint, spray texture, etc.) _____

Purchased From _____ Date _____

Brand & Pattern _____

Color & No. _____ Warranty Period _____

Applied with (texture roller, sprayer, etc.) _____

Cost/Unit $_____ No. of Units _____ Total $_____

Installed By _____

Date _____ Cost $_____

Notes: _____

_____

WINDOW COVERING

Window 1 Measurements

Height _____ Width _____ Top of Window to Floor _____

Type of Covering (draperies, blinds, etc.) _____

Purchased From _____ Cost $_____ Date _____

Measurements of Window Covering _____

Fabric & Cleaning Instructions _____

Cleaned By _____ Cost $_____ Date _____

Notes: _____

Window 2 Measurements

Height _____ Width _____ Top of Window to Floor _____

Type of Covering (draperies, blinds, etc.) _____

Purchased From _____ Cost $_____ Date _____

Measurements of Window Covering _____

Fabric & Cleaning Instructions _____

Cleaned By _____ Cost $_____ Date _____

Notes: _____

WALL COVERING

Wall Measurements

North _____ South _____ East _____ West _____

Note: Use "2nd Type of Covering" for woodwork or panelling. It has a "Refinished By" section.

1st Type of Covering (paint, paper, etc.) _____

Purchased From _____ Date _____

Brand & Pattern _____

Color & No. _____ Warranty Period _____

Cost/Unit $_____ No. of Units _____ Total $_____

Installed By _____

Date _____ Cost $_____

Notes: _____

WALL COVERING (continued)

2nd Type of Covering (woodwork, panelling, etc.) _____

Purchased From _____ Date _____

   Brand & Pattern _____

   Color & No. _____ Warranty Period _____

   Cost/Unit $_____ No. of Units _____ Total $_____

Installed By _____

   Date _____ Cost $_____

Refinished By _____

   Date _____ Cost $_____

Notes: _____

SAMPLES: PAINT, WALLPAPER, ETC.

attach swatch or paint daub here

FURNITURE/APPLIANCES

Item	Purchased From	Date	Cost	Warranty

EXTRA NOTES

(Use tick marks at top & bottom to make graph paper)

BATHROOM NUMBER 3
FLOOR COVERING

Floor Measurements

Widest part of room from middle of doorway _____

Longest part of room from middle of doorway _____

Notes: _____

Type of Covering (carpet, tile, etc.) _____

Purchased From _____ Date _____

Brand & Pattern _____

Color & No. _____ Warranty Period _____

Type of Backing _____ Pad Type _____

Cost/Unit $_____ No. of Units _____ Total $_____

Installed By _____ Attached With _____

Date _____ Cost $_____

Cleaned/Refinished By _____

Date 1 _____ Cost $_____

Date 2 _____ Cost $_____

Notes: _____

_____

CEILING COVERING

Type of Covering (paint, spray texture, etc.) _____

Purchased From _____ Date _____

Brand & Pattern _____

Color & No. _____ Warranty Period _____

Applied with (texture roller, sprayer, etc.) _____

Cost/Unit $_____ No. of Units _____ Total $_____

Installed By _____

Date _____ Cost $_____

Notes: _____

_____

WINDOW COVERING

Window 1 Measurements

Height _____ Width _____ Top of Window to Floor _____

Type of Covering (draperies, blinds, etc.) _____

Purchased From _____ Cost $_____ Date _____

    Measurements of Window Covering _____

    Fabric & Cleaning Instructions _____

Cleaned By _____ Cost $_____ Date _____

Notes: _____

Window 2 Measurements

Height _____ Width _____ Top of Window to Floor _____

Type of Covering (draperies, blinds, etc.) _____

Purchased From _____ Cost $_____ Date _____

    Measurements of Window Covering _____

    Fabric & Cleaning Instructions _____

Cleaned By _____ Cost $_____ Date _____

Notes: _____

WALL COVERING

Wall Measurements

North _____ South _____ East _____ West _____

Note: Use "2nd Type of Covering" for woodwork or panelling. It has a "Refinished By" section.

1st Type of Covering (paint, paper, etc.) _____

Purchased From _____ Date _____

    Brand & Pattern _____

    Color & No. _____ Warranty Period _____

    Cost/Unit $_____ No. of Units _____ Total $_____

Installed By _____

    Date _____ Cost $_____

Notes: _____

WALL COVERING (continued)

2nd Type of Covering (woodwork, panelling, etc.) _____

Purchased From _____ Date _____

   Brand & Pattern _____

   Color & No. _____ Warranty Period _____

   Cost/Unit $_____ No. of Units _____ Total $_____

Installed By _____

   Date _____ Cost $_____

Refinished By _____

   Date _____ Cost $_____

Notes: _____

SAMPLES: PAINT, WALLPAPER, ETC.

attach swatch or paint daub here

FURNITURE/APPLIANCES

Item	Purchased From	Date	Cost	Warranty

<u>EXTRA NOTES</u>

(Use tick marks at top & bottom to make graph paper)

BEDROOM NUMBER 1
FLOOR COVERING

Floor Measurements

Widest part of room from middle of doorway _____

Longest part of room from middle of doorway _____

Notes: _____

Type of Covering (carpet, hardwood, etc.) _____

Purchased From _____ Date _____

Brand & Pattern _____

Color & No. _____ Warranty Period _____

Type of Backing _____ Pad Type _____

Cost/Unit $_____ No. of Units _____ Total $_____

Installed By _____ Attached With _____

Date _____ Cost $_____

Cleaned/Refinished By _____

Date 1 _____ Cost $_____

Date 2 _____ Cost $_____

Notes: _____

_____

CEILING COVERING

Type of Covering (paint, spray texture, etc.) _____

Purchased From _____ Date _____

Brand & Pattern _____

Color & No. _____ Warranty Period _____

Applied with (texture roller, sprayer, etc.) _____

Cost/Unit $_____ No. of Units _____ Total $_____

Installed By _____

Date _____ Cost $_____

Notes: _____

_____

WINDOW COVERING

Window 1 Measurements

Height _____ Width _____ Top of Window to Floor _____

Type of Covering (draperies, blinds, etc.) _____

Purchased From _____ Cost $_____ Date _____

Measurements of Window Covering _____

Fabric & Cleaning Instructions _____

Cleaned By _____ Cost $_____ Date _____

Notes: _____

_____

Window 2 Measurements

Height _____ Width _____ Top of Window to Floor _____

Type of Covering (draperies, blinds, etc.) _____

Purchased From _____ Cost $_____ Date _____

Measurements of Window Covering _____

Fabric & Cleaning Instructions _____

Cleaned By _____ Cost $_____ Date _____

Notes: _____

_____

Window 3 Measurements

Height _____ Width _____ Top of Window to Floor _____

Type of Covering (draperies, blinds, etc.) _____

Purchased From _____ Cost $_____ Date _____

Measurements of Window Covering _____

Fabric & Cleaning Instructions _____

Cleaned By _____ Cost $_____ Date _____

Notes: _____

_____

Window 4 Measurements

Height _____ Width _____ Top of Window to Floor _____

Type of Covering (draperies, blinds, etc.) _____

Purchased From _____ Cost $_____ Date _____

Measurements of Window Covering _____

Fabric & Cleaning Instructions _____

Cleaned By _____ Cost $_____ Date _____

WALL COVERING

Wall Measurements

North _____ South _____ East _____ West _____

Note: Use "2nd Type of Covering" for woodwork or panelling. It has a "Refinished By" section.

1st Type of Covering (paint, paper, etc.) _____

Purchased From _____ Date _____

Brand & Pattern _____

Color & No. _____ Warranty Period _____

Cost/Unit $_____ No. of Units _____ Total $_____

Installed By _____

Date _____ Cost $_____

Notes: _____

2nd Type of Covering (woodwork, panelling, etc.) _____

Purchased From _____ Date _____

Brand & Pattern _____

Color & No. _____ Warranty Period _____

Cost/Unit $_____ No. of Units _____ Total $_____

Installed By _____

Date _____ Cost $_____

Refinished By _____

Date _____ Cost $_____

Notes: _____

SAMPLES: PAINT, WALLPAPER, ETC.

attach swatch or paint daub here

FURNITURE/APPLIANCES

Item	Purchased From	Date	Cost	Warranty

<u>EXTRA NOTES</u>

(Use tick marks at top & bottom to make graph paper)

BEDROOM NUMBER 2

FLOOR COVERING

Floor Measurements

Widest part of room from middle of doorway _____

Longest part of room from middle of doorway _____

Notes: _____

Type of Covering (carpet, hardwood, etc.) _____

Purchased From _____ Date _____

Brand & Pattern _____

Color & No. _____ Warranty Period _____

Type of Backing _____ Pad Type _____

Cost/Unit $_____ No. of Units _____ Total $_____

Installed By _____ Attached With _____

Date _____ Cost $_____

Cleaned/Refinished By _____

Date 1 _____ Cost $_____

Date 2 _____ Cost $_____

Notes: _____

_____

CEILING COVERING

Type of Covering (paint, spray texture, etc.) _____

Purchased From _____ Date _____

Brand & Pattern _____

Color & No. _____ Warranty Period _____

Applied with (texture roller, sprayer, etc.) _____

Cost/Unit $_____ No. of Units _____ Total $_____

Installed By _____

Date _____ Cost $_____

Notes: _____

_____

WINDOW COVERING

Window 1 Measurements

Height _____ Width _____ Top of Window to Floor _____

Type of Covering (draperies, blinds, etc.) _____

Purchased From _____ Cost $_____ Date _____

    Measurements of Window Covering _____

    Fabric & Cleaning Instructions _____

Cleaned By _____ Cost $_____ Date _____

Notes: _____

_____

Window 2 Measurements

Height _____ Width _____ Top of Window to Floor _____

Type of Covering (draperies, blinds, etc.) _____

Purchased From _____ Cost $_____ Date _____

    Measurements of Window Covering _____

    Fabric & Cleaning Instructions _____

Cleaned By _____ Cost $_____ Date _____

Notes: _____

_____

Window 3 Measurements

Height _____ Width _____ Top of Window to Floor _____

Type of Covering (draperies, blinds, etc.) _____

Purchased From _____ Cost $_____ Date _____

    Measurements of Window Covering _____

    Fabric & Cleaning Instructions _____

Cleaned By _____ Cost $_____ Date _____

Notes: _____

_____

Window 4 Measurements

Height _____ Width _____ Top of Window to Floor _____

Type of Covering (draperies, blinds, etc.) _____

Purchased From _____ Cost $_____ Date _____

    Measurements of Window Covering _____

    Fabric & Cleaning Instructions _____

Cleaned By _____ Cost $_____ Date _____

WALL COVERING

Wall Measurements

North _____ South _____ East _____ West _____

Note: Use "2nd Type of Covering" for woodwork or panelling. It has a "Refinished By" section.

1st Type of Covering (paint, paper, etc.) _____

Purchased From _____ Date _____

    Brand & Pattern _____

    Color & No. _____ Warranty Period _____

    Cost/Unit $_____ No. of Units _____ Total $_____

Installed By _____

    Date _____ Cost $_____

Notes: _____

2nd Type of Covering (woodwork, panelling, etc.) _____

Purchased From _____ Date _____

    Brand & Pattern _____

    Color & No. _____ Warranty Period _____

    Cost/Unit $_____ No. of Units _____ Total $_____

Installed By _____

    Date _____ Cost $_____

Refinished By _____

    Date _____ Cost $_____

Notes: _____

SAMPLES: PAINT, WALLPAPER, ETC.

attach swatch or paint daub here

FURNITURE/APPLIANCES

Item	Purchased From	Date	Cost	Warranty

EXTRA NOTES

(Use tick marks at top & bottom to make graph paper)

BEDROOM NUMBER 3
FLOOR COVERING

Floor Measurements

Widest part of room from middle of doorway _____

Longest part of room from middle of doorway _____

Notes: _____

Type of Covering (carpet, hardwood, etc.) _____

Purchased From _____ Date _____

Brand & Pattern _____

Color & No. _____ Warranty Period _____

Type of Backing _____ Pad Type _____

Cost/Unit $_____ No. of Units _____ Total $_____

Installed By _____ Attached With _____

Date _____ Cost $_____

Cleaned/Refinished By _____

Date 1 _____ Cost $_____

Date 2 _____ Cost $_____

Notes: _____

_____

CEILING COVERING

Type of Covering (paint, spray texture, etc.) _____

Purchased From _____ Date _____

Brand & Pattern _____

Color & No. _____ Warranty Period _____

Applied with (texture roller, sprayer, etc.) _____

Cost/Unit $_____ No. of Units _____ Total $_____

Installed By _____

Date _____ Cost $_____

Notes: _____

_____

WINDOW COVERING

Window 1 Measurements

Height _____ Width _____ Top of Window to Floor _____

Type of Covering (draperies, blinds, etc.) _____

Purchased From _____ Cost $_____ Date _____

    Measurements of Window Covering _____

    Fabric & Cleaning Instructions _____

Cleaned By _____ Cost $_____ Date _____

Notes: _____

_____

Window 2 Measurements

Height _____ Width _____ Top of Window to Floor _____

Type of Covering (draperies, blinds, etc.) _____

Purchased From _____ Cost $_____ Date _____

    Measurements of Window Covering _____

    Fabric & Cleaning Instructions _____

Cleaned By _____ Cost $_____ Date _____

Notes: _____

_____

Window 3 Measurements

Height _____ Width _____ Top of Window to Floor _____

Type of Covering (draperies, blinds, etc.) _____

Purchased From _____ Cost $_____ Date _____

    Measurements of Window Covering _____

    Fabric & Cleaning Instructions _____

Cleaned By _____ Cost $_____ Date _____

Notes: _____

_____

Window 4 Measurements

Height _____ Width _____ Top of Window to Floor _____

Type of Covering (draperies, blinds, etc.) _____

Purchased From _____ Cost $_____ Date _____

    Measurements of Window Covering _____

    Fabric & Cleaning Instructions _____

Cleaned By _____ Cost $_____ Date _____

WALL COVERING

Wall Measurements

North _____ South _____ East _____ West _____

Note: Use "2nd Type of Covering" for woodwork or panelling. It has a "Refinished By" section.

1st Type of Covering (paint, paper, etc.) _____

Purchased From _____ Date _____

    Brand & Pattern _____

    Color & No. _____ Warranty Period _____

    Cost/Unit $_____ No. of Units _____ Total $_____

Installed By _____

    Date _____ Cost $_____

Notes: _____

2nd Type of Covering (woodwork, panelling, etc.) _____

Purchased From _____ Date _____

    Brand & Pattern _____

    Color & No. _____ Warranty Period _____

    Cost/Unit $_____ No. of Units _____ Total $_____

Installed By _____ _____

    Date _____ Cost $_____

Refinished By _____

    Date _____ Cost $_____

Notes: _____

SAMPLES: PAINT, WALLPAPER, ETC.

attach swatch or paint daub here

FURNITURE/APPLIANCES

Item	Purchased From	Date	Cost	Warranty

EXTRA NOTES

(Use tick marks at top & bottom to make graph paper)

BEDROOM NUMBER 4
FLOOR COVERING

Floor Measurements

Widest part of room from middle of doorway _____

Longest part of room from middle of doorway _____

Notes: _____

Type of Covering (carpet, hardwood, etc.) _____

Purchased From _____ Date _____

Brand & Pattern _____

Color & No. _____ Warranty Period _____

Type of Backing _____ Pad Type _____

Cost/Unit $_____ No. of Units _____ Total $_____

Installed By _____ Attached With _____

Date _____ Cost $_____

Cleaned/Refinished By _____

Date 1 _____ Cost $_____

Date 2 _____ Cost $_____

Notes: _____

_____

CEILING COVERING

Type of Covering (paint, spray texture, etc.) _____

Purchased From _____ Date _____

Brand & Pattern _____

Color & No. _____ Warranty Period _____

Applied with (texture roller, sprayer, etc.) _____

Cost/Unit $_____ No. of Units _____ Total $_____

Installed By _____

Date _____ Cost $_____

Notes: _____

_____

WINDOW COVERING

Window 1 Measurements

Height _____ Width _____ Top of Window to Floor _____

Type of Covering (draperies, blinds, etc.) _____

Purchased From _____ Cost $_____ Date _____

Measurements of Window Covering _____

Fabric & Cleaning Instructions _____

Cleaned By _____ Cost $_____ Date _____

Notes: _____

_____

Window 2 Measurements

Height _____ Width _____ Top of Window to Floor _____

Type of Covering (draperies, blinds, etc.) _____

Purchased From _____ Cost $_____ Date _____

Measurements of Window Covering _____

Fabric & Cleaning Instructions _____

Cleaned By _____ Cost $_____ Date _____

Notes: _____

_____

Window 3 Measurements

Height _____ Width _____ Top of Window to Floor _____

Type of Covering (draperies, blinds, etc.) _____

Purchased From _____ Cost $_____ Date _____

Measurements of Window Covering _____

Fabric & Cleaning Instructions _____

Cleaned By _____ Cost $_____ Date _____

Notes: _____

_____

Window 4 Measurements

Height _____ Width _____ Top of Window to Floor _____

Type of Covering (draperies, blinds, etc.) _____

Purchased From _____ Cost $_____ Date _____

    Measurements of Window Covering _____

    Fabric & Cleaning Instructions _____

Cleaned By _____ Cost $_____ Date _____

WALL COVERING

Wall Measurements

North _____ South _____ East _____ West _____

Note: Use "2nd Type of Covering" for woodwork or panelling. It has a "Refinished By" section.

1st Type of Covering (paint, paper, etc.) _____

Purchased From _____ Date _____

    Brand & Pattern _____

    Color & No. _____ Warranty Period _____

    Cost/Unit $_____ No. of Units _____ Total $_____

Installed By _____

    Date _____ Cost $_____

Notes: _____

2nd Type of Covering (woodwork, panelling, etc.) _____

Purchased From _____ Date _____

    Brand & Pattern _____

    Color & No. _____ Warranty Period _____

    Cost/Unit $_____ No. of Units _____ Total $_____

Installed By _____

    Date _____ Cost $_____

Refinished By _____

    Date _____ Cost $_____

Notes: _____

SAMPLES: PAINT, WALLPAPER, ETC.

attach swatch or paint daub here

FURNITURE/APPLIANCES

Item	Purchased From	Date	Cost	Warranty

EXTRA NOTES

(Use tick marks at top & bottom to make graph paper)

DEN/STUDY/OFFICE
FLOOR COVERING

Floor Measurements

Widest part of room from middle of doorway _____

Longest part of room from middle of doorway _____

Notes: _____

Type of Covering (carpet, hardwood, etc.) _____

Purchased From _____ Date _____

Brand & Pattern _____

Color & No. _____ Warranty Period _____

Type of Backing _____ Pad Type _____

Cost/Unit $_____ No. of Units _____ Total $_____

Installed By _____ Attached With _____

Date _____ Cost $_____

Cleaned/Refinished By _____

Date 1 _____ Cost $_____

Date 2 _____ Cost $_____

Notes: _____

_____

CEILING COVERING

Type of Covering (paint, spray texture, etc.) _____

Purchased From _____ Date _____

Brand & Pattern _____

Color & No. _____ Warranty Period _____

Applied with (texture roller, sprayer, etc.) _____

Cost/Unit $_____ No. of Units _____ Total $_____

Installed By _____

Date _____ Cost $_____

Notes: _____

_____

WINDOW COVERING

Window 1 Measurements

Height _____ Width _____ Top of Window to Floor _____

Type of Covering (draperies, blinds, etc.) _____

Purchased From _____ Cost $_____ Date _____

Measurements of Window Covering _____

Fabric & Cleaning Instructions _____

Cleaned By _____ Cost $_____ Date _____

Notes: _____

_____

Window 2 Measurements

Height _____ Width _____ Top of Window to Floor _____

Type of Covering (draperies, blinds, etc.) _____

Purchased From _____ Cost $_____ Date _____

Measurements of Window Covering _____

Fabric & Cleaning Instructions _____

Cleaned By _____ Cost $_____ Date _____

Notes: _____

_____

Window 3 Measurements

Height _____ Width _____ Top of Window to Floor _____

Type of Covering (draperies, blinds, etc.) _____

Purchased From _____ Cost $_____ Date _____

Measurements of Window Covering _____

Fabric & Cleaning Instructions _____

Cleaned By _____ Cost $_____ Date _____

Notes: _____

_____

Window 4 Measurements

Height _____ Width _____ Top of Window to Floor _____

Type of Covering (draperies, blinds, etc.) _____

Purchased From _____ Cost $_____ Date _____

    Measurements of Window Covering _____

    Fabric & Cleaning Instructions _____

Cleaned By _____ Cost $_____ Date _____

WALL COVERING

Wall Measurements

North _____ South _____ East _____ West _____

Note: Use "2nd Type of Covering" for woodwork or panelling. It has a "Refinished By" section.

1st Type of Covering (paint, paper, etc.) _____

Purchased From _____ Date _____

    Brand & Pattern _____

    Color & No. _____ Warranty Period _____

    Cost/Unit $_____ No. of Units _____ Total $_____

Installed By _____

    Date _____ Cost $_____

Notes: _____

2nd Type of Covering (woodwork, panelling, etc.) _____

Purchased From _____ Date _____

    Brand & Pattern _____

    Color & No. _____ Warranty Period _____

    Cost/Unit $_____ No. of Units _____ Total $_____

Installed By _____

    Date _____ Cost $_____

Refinished By _____

    Date _____ Cost $_____

Notes: _____

SAMPLES: PAINT, WALLPAPER, ETC.

attach swatch or paint daub here

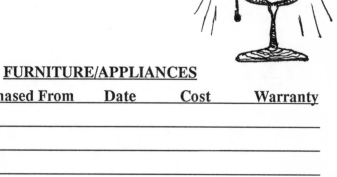

FURNITURE/APPLIANCES

Item	Purchased From	Date	Cost	Warranty

EXTRA NOTES

(Use tick marks at top & bottom to make graph paper)

DINING ROOM
FLOOR COVERING

Floor Measurements

Widest part of room from middle of doorway _____

Longest part of room from middle of doorway _____

Notes: _____

Type of Covering (carpet, hardwood, etc.) _____

Purchased From _____ Date _____

Brand & Pattern _____

Color & No. _____ Warranty Period _____

Type of Backing _____ Pad Type _____

Cost/Unit $_____ No. of Units _____ Total $_____

Installed By _____ Attached With _____

Date _____ Cost $_____

Cleaned/Refinished By _____

Date 1 _____ Cost $_____

Date 2 _____ Cost $_____

Notes: _____

_____

CEILING COVERING

Type of Covering (paint, spray texture, etc.) _____

Purchased From _____ Date _____

Brand & Pattern _____

Color & No. _____ Warranty Period _____

Applied with (texture roller, sprayer, etc.) _____

Cost/Unit $_____ No. of Units _____ Total $_____

Installed By _____

Date _____ Cost $_____

Notes: _____

_____

WINDOW COVERING

Window 1 Measurements

Height _____ Width _____ Top of Window to Floor _____

Type of Covering (draperies, blinds, etc.) _____

Purchased From _____ Cost $_____ Date _____

Measurements of Window Covering _____

Fabric & Cleaning Instructions _____

Cleaned By _____ Cost $_____ Date _____

Notes: _____

_____

Window 2 Measurements

Height _____ Width _____ Top of Window to Floor _____

Type of Covering (draperies, blinds, etc.) _____

Purchased From _____ Cost $_____ Date _____

Measurements of Window Covering _____

Fabric & Cleaning Instructions _____

Cleaned By _____ Cost $_____ Date _____

Notes: _____

_____

Window 3 Measurements

Height _____ Width _____ Top of Window to Floor _____

Type of Covering (draperies, blinds, etc.) _____

Purchased From _____ Cost $_____ Date _____

Measurements of Window Covering _____

Fabric & Cleaning Instructions _____

Cleaned By _____ Cost $_____ Date _____

Notes: _____

_____

Window 4 Measurements

Height _____ Width _____ Top of Window to Floor _____

Type of Covering (draperies, blinds, etc.) _____

Purchased From _____ Cost $_____ Date _____

Measurements of Window Covering _____

Fabric & Cleaning Instructions _____

Cleaned By _____ Cost $_____ Date _____

WALL COVERING

Wall Measurements

North _____ South _____ East _____ West _____

Note: Use "2nd Type of Covering" for woodwork or panelling. It has a "Refinished By" section.

1st Type of Covering (paint, paper, etc.) _____

Purchased From _____ Date _____

Brand & Pattern _____

Color & No. _____ Warranty Period _____

Cost/Unit $_____ No. of Units _____ Total $_____

Installed By _____

Date _____ Cost $_____

Notes: _____

2nd Type of Covering (woodwork, panelling, etc.) _____

Purchased From _____ Date _____

Brand & Pattern _____

Color & No. _____ Warranty Period _____

Cost/Unit $_____ No. of Units _____ Total $_____

Installed By _____

Date _____ Cost $_____

Refinished By _____

Date _____ Cost $_____

Notes: _____

SAMPLES: PAINT, WALLPAPER, ETC.

attach swatch or paint daub here

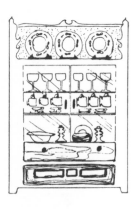

FURNITURE/APPLIANCES

Item	Purchased From	Date	Cost	Warranty

EXTRA NOTES

(Use tick marks at top & bottom to make graph paper)

ELECTRICAL/WIRING

Suggestion: Use tick marks at top & bottom to make graph paper. Sketch the layout of your fuse box. Label the fuses and identify the outlets and appliances they control.

ENTRY/FOYER/MUD ROOM
FLOOR COVERING

Floor Measurements

Widest part of room from middle of doorway _____

Longest part of room from middle of doorway _____

Notes: _____

Type of Covering (carpet, tile, etc.) _____

Purchased From _____ Date _____

Brand & Pattern _____

Color & No. _____ Warranty Period _____

Type of Backing _____ Pad Type _____

Cost/Unit $_____ No. of Units _____ Total $_____

Installed By _____ Attached With _____

Date _____ Cost $_____

Cleaned/Refinished By _____

Date 1 _____ Cost $_____

Date 2 _____ Cost $_____

Notes: _____

_____

CEILING COVERING

Type of Covering (paint, spray texture, etc.) _____

Purchased From _____ Date _____

Brand & Pattern _____

Color & No. _____ Warranty Period _____

Applied with (texture roller, sprayer, etc.) _____

Cost/Unit $_____ No. of Units _____ Total $_____

Installed By _____

Date _____ Cost $_____

Notes: _____

_____

WINDOW COVERING

Window Measurements

Height _____ Width _____ Top of Window to Floor ____

Type of Covering (draperies, blinds, etc.) _____

Purchased From _____ Cost $_____ Date _____

Measurements of Window Covering _____

Fabric & Cleaning Instructions _____

Cleaned By _____ Cost $_____ Date _____

Notes: _____

WALL COVERING

Wall Measurements

North _____ South _____ East _____ West _____

Note: Use "2nd Type of Covering" for woodwork or panelling. It has a "Refinished By" section.

1st Type of Covering (paint, paper, etc.) _____

Purchased From _____ Date _____

Brand & Pattern _____

Color & No. _____ Warranty Period _____

Cost/Unit $_____ No. of Units _____ Total $_____

Installed By _____

Date _____ Cost $_____

Notes: _____

2nd Type of Covering (woodwork, panelling, etc.) _____

Purchased From _____ Date _____

Brand & Pattern _____

Color & No. _____ Warranty Period _____

Cost/Unit $_____ No. of Units _____ Total $_____

Installed By _____

Date _____ Cost $_____

Refinished By _____

Date _____ Cost $_____

SAMPLES: PAINT, WALLPAPER, ETC.

attach swatch or paint daub here

FURNITURE

Item	Purchased From	Date	Cost	Warranty

EXTRA NOTES

FAMILY ROOM
FLOOR COVERING

Floor Measurements

Widest part of room from middle of doorway _____

Longest part of room from middle of doorway _____

Notes: _____

Type of Covering (carpet, hardwood, etc.) _____

Purchased From _____ Date _____

Brand & Pattern _____

Color & No. _____ Warranty Period _____

Type of Backing _____ Pad Type _____

Cost/Unit $_____ No. of Units _____ Total $_____

Installed By _____ Attached With _____

Date _____ Cost $_____

Cleaned/Refinished By _____

Date 1 _____ Cost $_____

Date 2 _____ Cost $_____

Notes: _____

_____

CEILING COVERING

Type of Covering (paint, spray texture, etc.) _____

Purchased From _____ Date _____

Brand & Pattern _____

Color & No. _____ Warranty Period _____

Applied with (texture roller, sprayer, etc.) _____

Cost/Unit $_____ No. of Units _____ Total $_____

Installed By _____

Date _____ Cost $_____

Notes: _____

_____

WINDOW COVERING

Window 1 Measurements

Height _____ Width _____ Top of Window to Floor ____

Type of Covering (draperies, blinds, etc.) _____

Purchased From _____ Cost $_____ Date _____

   Measurements of Window Covering _____

   Fabric & Cleaning Instructions _____

Cleaned By _____ Cost $_____ Date _____

Notes: _____

_____

Window 2 Measurements

Height _____ Width _____ Top of Window to Floor _____

Type of Covering (draperies, blinds, etc.) _____

Purchased From _____ Cost $_____ Date _____

   Measurements of Window Covering _____

   Fabric & Cleaning Instructions _____

Cleaned By _____ Cost $_____ Date _____

Notes: _____

_____

Window 3 Measurements

Height _____ Width _____ Top of Window to Floor _____

Type of Covering (draperies, blinds, etc.) _____

Purchased From _____ Cost $_____ Date _____

   Measurements of Window Covering _____

   Fabric & Cleaning Instructions _____

Cleaned By _____ Cost $_____ Date _____

Notes: _____

_____

Window 4 Measurements

Height _____ Width _____ Top of Window to Floor _____

Type of Covering (draperies, blinds, etc.) _____

Purchased From _____ Cost $_____ Date _____

 Measurements of Window Covering _____

 Fabric & Cleaning Instructions _____

Cleaned By _____ Cost $_____ Date _____

WALL COVERING

Wall Measurements

North _____ South _____ East _____ West _____

Note: Use "2nd Type of Covering" for woodwork or panelling. It has a "Refinished By" section.

1st Type of Covering (paint, paper, etc.) _____

Purchased From _____ Date _____

 Brand & Pattern _____

 Color & No. _____ Warranty Period _____

 Cost/Unit $_____ No. of Units _____ Total $_____

Installed By _____

 Date _____ Cost $_____

Notes: _____

2nd Type of Covering (woodwork, panelling, etc.) _____

Purchased From _____ Date _____

 Brand & Pattern _____

 Color & No. _____ Warranty Period _____

 Cost/Unit $_____ No. of Units _____ Total $_____

Installed By _____

 Date _____ Cost $_____

Refinished By _____

 Date _____ Cost $_____

Notes: _____

SAMPLES: PAINT, WALLPAPER, ETC.

attach swatch or paint daub here

FURNITURE/APPLIANCES

Item	Purchased From	Date	Cost	Warranty

EXTRA NOTES

(Use tick marks at top & bottom to make graph paper)

HALLWAY/STAIRWAY 1
FLOOR COVERING

Floor Measurements

Widest part of room from middle of doorway _____

Longest part of room from middle of doorway _____

Notes: _____

Type of Covering (carpet, tile, etc.) _____

Purchased From _____ Date _____

Brand & Pattern _____

Color & No. _____ Warranty Period _____

Type of Backing _____ Pad Type _____

Cost/Unit $_____ No. of Units _____ Total $_____

Installed By _____ Attached With _____

Date _____ Cost $_____

Cleaned/Refinished By _____

Date 1 _____ Cost $_____

Date 2 _____ Cost $_____

Notes: _____

_____

CEILING COVERING

Type of Covering (paint, spray texture, etc.) _____

Purchased From _____ Date _____

Brand & Pattern _____

Color & No. _____ Warranty Period _____

Applied with (texture roller, sprayer, etc.) _____

Cost/Unit $_____ No. of Units _____ Total $_____

Installed By _____

Date _____ Cost $_____

Notes: _____

_____

WINDOW COVERING

Window Measurements

Height _____ Width _____ Top of Window to Floor _____

Type of Covering (draperies, blinds, etc.) _____

Purchased From _____ Cost $_____ Date _____

    Measurements of Window Covering _____

    Fabric & Cleaning Instructions _____

Cleaned By _____ Cost $_____ Date _____

Notes: _____

WALL COVERING

Wall Measurements

North _____ South _____ East _____ West _____

Note: Use "2nd Type of Covering" for woodwork or panelling. It has a "Refinished By" section.

1st Type of Covering (paint, paper, etc.) _____

Purchased From _____ Date _____

    Brand & Pattern _____

    Color & No. _____ Warranty Period _____

    Cost/Unit $_____ No. of Units _____ Total $_____

Installed By _____

    Date _____ Cost $_____

Notes: _____

2nd Type of Covering (woodwork, panelling, etc.) _____

Purchased From _____ Date _____

    Brand & Pattern _____

    Color & No. _____ Warranty Period _____

    Cost/Unit $_____ No. of Units _____ Total $_____

Installed By _____

    Date _____ Cost $_____

Refinished By _____

    Date _____ Cost $_____

SAMPLES: PAINT, WALLPAPER, ETC.

attach swatch or paint daub here

EXTRA NOTES

_____

_____

_____

_____

_____

_____

_____

_____

_____

_____

_____

_____

_____

_____

HALLWAY/STAIRWAY 2
FLOOR COVERING

Floor Measurements

Widest part of room from middle of doorway _____

Longest part of room from middle of doorway _____

Notes: _____

Type of Covering (carpet, tile, etc.) _____

Purchased From _____ Date _____

Brand & Pattern _____

Color & No. _____ Warranty Period _____

Type of Backing _____ Pad Type _____

Cost/Unit $_____ No. of Units _____ Total $_____

Installed By _____ Attached With _____

Date _____ Cost $_____

Cleaned/Refinished By _____

Date 1 _____ Cost $_____

Date 2 _____ Cost $_____

Notes: _____

_____

CEILING COVERING

Type of Covering (paint, spray texture, etc.) _____

Purchased From _____ Date _____

Brand & Pattern _____

Color & No. _____ Warranty Period _____

Applied with (texture roller, sprayer, etc.) _____

Cost/Unit $_____ No. of Units _____ Total $_____

Installed By _____

Date _____ Cost $_____

Notes: _____

_____

WINDOW COVERING

Window Measurements

Height _____ Width _____ Top of Window to Floor _____

Type of Covering (draperies, blinds, etc.) _____

Purchased From _____ Cost $_____ Date _____

   Measurements of Window Covering _____

   Fabric & Cleaning Instructions _____

Cleaned By _____ Cost $_____ Date _____

Notes: _____

WALL COVERING

Wall Measurements

North _____ South _____ East _____ West _____

Note: Use "2nd Type of Covering" for woodwork or panelling. It has a "Refinished By" section.

1st Type of Covering (paint, paper, etc.) _____

Purchased From _____ Date _____

   Brand & Pattern _____

   Color & No. _____ Warranty Period _____

   Cost/Unit $_____ No. of Units _____ Total $_____

Installed By _____

   Date _____ Cost $_____

Notes: _____

2nd Type of Covering (woodwork, panelling, etc.) _____

Purchased From _____ Date _____

   Brand & Pattern _____

   Color & No. _____ Warranty Period _____

   Cost/Unit $_____ No. of Units _____ Total $_____

Installed By _____

   Date _____ Cost $_____

Refinished By _____

   Date _____ Cost $_____

SAMPLES: PAINT, WALLPAPER, ETC.

attach swatch or paint daub here

EXTRA NOTES

HALLWAY/STAIRWAY 3

FLOOR COVERING

Floor Measurements

Widest part of room from middle of doorway _____

Longest part of room from middle of doorway _____

Notes: _____

Type of Covering (carpet, tile, etc.) _____

Purchased From _____ Date _____

Brand & Pattern _____

Color & No. _____ Warranty Period _____

Type of Backing _____ Pad Type _____

Cost/Unit $_____ No. of Units _____ Total $_____

Installed By _____ Attached With _____

Date _____ Cost $_____

Cleaned/Refinished By _____

Date 1 _____ Cost $_____

Date 2 _____ Cost $_____

Notes: _____

_____

CEILING COVERING

Type of Covering (paint, spray texture, etc.) _____

Purchased From _____ Date _____

Brand & Pattern _____

Color & No. _____ Warranty Period _____

Applied with (texture roller, sprayer, etc.) _____

Cost/Unit $_____ No. of Units _____ Total $_____

Installed By _____

Date _____ Cost $_____

Notes: _____

_____

WINDOW COVERING

Window Measurements

Height _____ Width _____ Top of Window to Floor _____

Type of Covering (draperies, blinds, etc.) _____

Purchased From _____ Cost $_____ Date _____

   Measurements of Window Covering _____

   Fabric & Cleaning Instructions _____

Cleaned By _____ Cost $_____ Date _____

Notes: _____

WALL COVERING

Wall Measurements

North _____ South _____ East _____ West _____

Note: Use "2nd Type of Covering" for woodwork or panelling. It has a "Refinished By" section.

1st Type of Covering (paint, paper, etc.) _____

Purchased From _____ Date _____

   Brand & Pattern _____

   Color & No. _____ Warranty Period _____

   Cost/Unit $_____ No. of Units _____ Total $_____

Installed By _____

   Date _____ Cost $_____

Notes: _____

2nd Type of Covering (woodwork, panelling, etc.) _____

Purchased From _____ Date _____

   Brand & Pattern _____

   Color & No. _____ Warranty Period _____

   Cost/Unit $_____ No. of Units _____ Total $_____

Installed By _____

   Date _____ Cost $_____

Refinished By _____

   Date _____ Cost $_____

SAMPLES: PAINT, WALLPAPER, ETC.

attach swatch or paint daub here

EXTRA NOTES

_____

_____

_____

_____

_____

_____

_____

_____

_____

_____

_____

_____

_____

_____

_____

_____

_____

_____

KITCHEN
FLOOR COVERING

Floor Measurements

Widest part of room from middle of doorway _____

Longest part of room from middle of doorway _____

Notes: _____

Type of Covering (carpet, tile, etc.) _____

Purchased From _____ Date _____

Brand & Pattern _____

Color & No. _____ Warranty Period _____

Type of Backing _____ Pad Type _____

Cost/Unit $_____ No. of Units _____ Total $_____

Installed By _____ Attached With _____

Date _____ Cost $_____

Cleaned/Refinished By _____

Date 1 _____ Cost $_____

Date 2 _____ Cost $_____

Notes: _____

_____

CEILING COVERING

Type of Covering (paint, spray texture, etc.) _____

Purchased From _____ Date _____

Brand & Pattern _____

Color & No. _____ Warranty Period _____

Applied with (texture roller, sprayer, etc.) _____

Cost/Unit $_____ No. of Units _____ Total $_____

Installed By _____

Date _____ Cost $_____

Notes: _____

_____

WINDOW COVERING

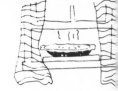

Window 1 Measurements

Height _____ Width _____ Top of Window to Floor _____

Type of Covering (draperies, blinds, etc.) _____

Purchased From _____ Cost $_____ Date _____

Measurements of Window Covering _____

Fabric & Cleaning Instructions _____

Cleaned By _____ Cost $_____ Date _____

Notes: _____

_____

Window 2 Measurements

Height _____ Width _____ Top of Window to Floor _____

Type of Covering (draperies, blinds, etc.) _____

Purchased From _____ Cost $_____ Date _____

Measurements of Window Covering _____

Fabric & Cleaning Instructions _____

Cleaned By _____ Cost $_____ Date _____

Notes: _____

_____

Window 3 Measurements

Height _____ Width _____ Top of Window to Floor _____

Type of Covering (draperies, blinds, etc.) _____

Purchased From _____ Cost $_____ Date _____

Measurements of Window Covering _____

Fabric & Cleaning Instructions _____

Cleaned By _____ Cost $_____ Date _____

Notes: _____

_____

Window 4 Measurements

Height _____ Width _____ Top of Window to Floor _____

Type of Covering (draperies, blinds, etc.) _____

Purchased From _____ Cost $_____ Date _____

   Measurements of Window Covering _____

   Fabric & Cleaning Instructions _____

Cleaned By _____ Cost $_____ Date _____

WALL COVERING

Wall Measurements

North _____ South _____ East _____ West _____

Note: Use "2nd Type of Covering" for woodwork or panelling. It has a "Refinished By" section.

1st Type of Covering (paint, paper, etc.) _____

Purchased From _____ Date _____

   Brand & Pattern _____

   Color & No. _____ Warranty Period _____

   Cost/Unit $_____ No. of Units _____ Total $_____

Installed By _____

   Date _____ Cost $_____

Notes: _____

2nd Type of Covering (woodwork, panelling, etc.) _____

Purchased From _____ Date _____

   Brand & Pattern _____

   Color & No. _____ Warranty Period _____

   Cost/Unit $_____ No. of Units _____ Total $_____

Installed By _____

   Date _____ Cost $_____

Refinished By _____

   Date _____ Cost $_____

Notes: _____

CABINETS

Purchased From _____ Date _____

   Brand & Style _____ Stain Color & No. _____

     Type of Wood (oak, pine, etc.) _____

     Finished With (polyurethane, varnish, etc.) _____

   Countertop Material (laminate, etc.) _____

     Brand & Pattern _____ Color & No. _____

Installed By _____ Total Cost $_____

Refinished By _____

   Refinished With _____

   Date _____ Cost $_____

Notes: _____

_____

SAMPLES: PAINT, WALLPAPER, ETC.

attach swatch or paint daub here

MAJOR APPLIANCES

Type of Appliance (range, dishwasher, etc.) _____

Purchased From _____ Date _____

   Manufacturer _____ Cost $_____

   Model/Lot/Serial No. _____

   Authorized Service Center _____ Warranty Period _____

<u>**Type of Appliance**</u> (range, dishwasher, etc.) _____

Purchased From _____ Date _____

    Manufacturer _____ Cost $_____

    Model/Lot/Serial No. _____

    Authorized Service Center _____ Warranty Period _____

<u>**Type of Appliance**</u> (range, dishwasher, etc.) _____

Purchased From _____ Date _____

    Manufacturer _____ Cost $_____

    Model/Lot/Serial No. _____

    Authorized Service Center _____ Warranty Period _____

<u>**Type of Appliance**</u> (range, dishwasher, etc.) _____

Purchased From _____ Date _____

    Manufacturer _____ Cost $_____

    Model/Lot/Serial No. _____

    Authorized Service Center _____ Warranty Period _____

<u>**Type of Appliance**</u> (range, dishwasher, etc.) _____

Purchased From _____ Date _____

    Manufacturer _____ Cost $_____

    Model/Lot/Serial No. _____

    Authorized Service Center _____ Warranty Period _____

FURNITURE/SMALL APPLIANCES

Item	Purchased From	Date	Cost	Warranty

<u>EXTRA NOTES</u>

(Use tick marks at top & bottom to make graph paper)

LAUNDRY ROOM
FLOOR COVERING

Floor Measurements

Widest part of room from middle of doorway _____

Longest part of room from middle of doorway _____

Notes: _____

Type of Covering (carpet, tile, etc.) _____

Purchased From _____ Date _____

Brand & Pattern _____

Color & No. _____ Warranty Period _____

Type of Backing _____ Pad Type _____

Cost/Unit $_____ No. of Units _____ Total $_____

Installed By _____ Attached With _____

Date _____ Cost $_____

Cleaned/Refinished By _____

Date 1 _____ Cost $_____

Date 2 _____ Cost $_____

Notes: _____

CEILING COVERING

Type of Covering (paint, spray texture, etc.) _____

Purchased From _____ Date _____

Brand & Pattern _____

Color & No. _____ Warranty Period _____

Applied with (texture roller, sprayer, etc.) _____

Cost/Unit $_____ No. of Units _____ Total $_____

Installed By _____

Date _____ Cost $_____

Notes: _____

WINDOW COVERING

Window Measurements

Height _____ Width _____ Top of Window to Floor _____

Type of Covering (draperies, blinds, etc.) _____

Purchased From _____ Cost $_____ Date _____

   Measurements of Window Covering _____

   Fabric & Cleaning Instructions _____

Cleaned By _____ Cost $_____ Date _____

Notes: _____

WALL COVERING

Wall Measurements

North _____ South _____ East _____ West _____

Note: Use "2nd Type of Covering" for woodwork or panelling. It has a "Refinished By" section.

1st Type of Covering (paint, paper, etc.) _____

Purchased From _____ Date _____

   Brand & Pattern _____

   Color & No. _____ Warranty Period _____

   Cost/Unit $_____ No. of Units _____ Total $_____

Installed By _____

   Date _____ Cost $_____

Notes: _____

2nd Type of Covering (woodwork, panelling, etc.) _____

Purchased From _____ Date _____

   Brand & Pattern _____

   Color & No. _____ Warranty Period _____

   Cost/Unit $_____ No. of Units _____ Total $_____

Installed By _____

   Date _____ Cost $_____

Refinished By _____

   Date _____ Cost $_____

SAMPLES: PAINT, WALLPAPER, ETC.

attach swatch or paint daub here

MAJOR APPLIANCES

Type of Appliance (washer, dryer, etc.) _____

Purchased From _____ Date _____

   Manufacturer _____ Cost $_____

   Model/Lot/Serial No. _____

   Authorized Service Center _____ Warranty Period _____

Type of Appliance (washer, dryer, etc.) _____

Purchased From _____ Date _____

   Manufacturer _____ Cost $_____

   Model/Lot/Serial No. _____

   Authorized Service Center _____ Warranty Period _____

Type of Appliance (washer, dryer, etc.) _____

Purchased From _____ Date _____

   Manufacturer _____ Cost $_____

   Model/Lot/Serial No. _____

   Authorized Service Center _____ Warranty Period _____

Type of Appliance (washer, dryer, etc.) _____

Purchased From _____ Date _____

   Manufacturer _____ Cost $_____

   Model/Lot/Serial No. _____

   Authorized Service Center _____ Warranty Period _____

LIVING ROOM
FLOOR COVERING

Floor Measurements

Widest part of room from middle of doorway _____

Longest part of room from middle of doorway _____

Notes: _____

Type of Covering (carpet, hardwood, etc.) _____

Purchased From _____ Date _____

Brand & Pattern _____

Color & No. _____ Warranty Period _____

Type of Backing _____ Pad Type _____

Cost/Unit $_____ No. of Units _____ Total $_____

Installed By _____ Attached With _____

Date _____ Cost $_____

Cleaned/Refinished By _____

Date 1 _____ Cost $_____

Date 2 _____ Cost $_____

Notes: _____ _____

_____

CEILING COVERING

Type of Covering (paint, spray texture, etc.) _____

Purchased From _____ Date _____

Brand & Pattern _____

Color & No. _____ Warranty Period _____

Applied with (texture roller, sprayer, etc.) _____

Cost/Unit $_____ No. of Units _____ Total $_____

Installed By _____

Date _____ Cost $_____

Notes: _____

_____

WINDOW COVERING

Window 1 Measurements

Height _____ Width _____ Top of Window to Floor _____

Type of Covering (draperies, blinds, etc.) _____

Purchased From _____ Cost $_____ Date _____

    Measurements of Window Covering _____

    Fabric & Cleaning Instructions _____

Cleaned By _____ Cost $_____ Date _____

Notes: _____

_____

Window 2 Measurements

Height _____ Width _____ Top of Window to Floor _____

Type of Covering (draperies, blinds, etc.) _____

Purchased From _____ Cost $_____ Date _____

    Measurements of Window Covering _____

    Fabric & Cleaning Instructions _____

Cleaned By _____ Cost $_____ Date _____

Notes: _____

_____

Window 3 Measurements

Height _____ Width _____ Top of Window to Floor _____

Type of Covering (draperies, blinds, etc.) _____

Purchased From _____ Cost $_____ Date _____

    Measurements of Window Covering _____

    Fabric & Cleaning Instructions _____

Cleaned By _____ Cost $_____ Date _____

Notes: _____

_____

<u>**Window 4 Measurements**</u>

   Height _____ Width _____ Top of Window to Floor _____

<u>**Type of Covering**</u> (draperies, blinds, etc.) _____

Purchased From _____ Cost $_____ Date _____

   Measurements of Window Covering _____

   Fabric & Cleaning Instructions _____

Cleaned By _____ Cost $_____ Date _____

WALL COVERING

<u>**Wall Measurements**</u>

North _____ South _____ East _____ West _____

Note: Use "2nd Type of Covering" for woodwork or panelling. It has a "Refinished By" section.

<u>**1st Type of Covering**</u> (paint, paper, etc.) _____

Purchased From _____ Date _____

   Brand & Pattern _____

   Color & No. _____ Warranty Period _____

   Cost/Unit $_____ No. of Units _____ Total $_____

Installed By _____

   Date _____ Cost $_____

Notes: _____

<u>**2nd Type of Covering**</u> (woodwork, panelling, etc.) _____

Purchased From _____ Date _____

   Brand & Pattern _____

   Color & No. _____ Warranty Period _____

   Cost/Unit $_____ No. of Units _____ Total $_____

Installed By _____

   Date _____ Cost $_____

Refinished By _____

   Date _____ Cost $_____

Notes: _____

SAMPLES: PAINT, WALLPAPER, ETC.

attach swatch or paint daub here

FURNITURE/APPLIANCES

Item	Purchased From	Date	Cost	Warranty

EXTRA NOTES

(Use tick marks at top & bottom to make graph paper)

MISCELLANEOUS ROOM 1
FLOOR COVERING

Floor Measurements

Widest part of room from middle of doorway _____

Longest part of room from middle of doorway _____

Notes: _____

Type of Covering (carpet, hardwood, etc.) _____

Purchased From _____ Date _____

Brand & Pattern _____

Color & No. _____ Warranty Period _____

Type of Backing _____ Pad Type _____

Cost/Unit $_____ No. of Units _____ Total $_____

Installed By _____ Attached With _____

Date _____ Cost $_____

Cleaned/Refinished By _____

Date 1 _____ Cost $_____

Date 2 _____ Cost $_____

Notes: _____

_____

CEILING COVERING

Type of Covering (paint, spray texture, etc.) _____

Purchased From _____ Date _____

Brand & Pattern _____

Color & No. _____ Warranty Period _____

Applied with (texture roller, sprayer, etc.) _____

Cost/Unit $_____ No. of Units _____ Total $_____

Installed By _____

Date _____ Cost $_____

Notes: _____

_____

WINDOW COVERING

Window 1 Measurements

Height _____ Width _____ Top of Window to Floor _____

Type of Covering (draperies, blinds, etc.) _____

Purchased From _____ Cost $_____ Date _____

   Measurements of Window Covering _____

   Fabric & Cleaning Instructions _____

Cleaned By _____ Cost $_____ Date _____

Notes: _____

_____

Window 2 Measurements

Height _____ Width _____ Top of Window to Floor _____

Type of Covering (draperies, blinds, etc.) _____

Purchased From _____ Cost $_____ Date _____

   Measurements of Window Covering _____

   Fabric & Cleaning Instructions _____

Cleaned By _____ Cost $_____ Date _____

Notes: _____

_____

Window 3 Measurements

Height _____ Width _____ Top of Window to Floor _____

Type of Covering (draperies, blinds, etc.) _____

Purchased From _____ Cost $_____ Date _____

   Measurements of Window Covering _____

   Fabric & Cleaning Instructions _____

Cleaned By _____ Cost $_____ Date _____

Notes: _____

_____

Window 4 Measurements

Height _____ Width _____ Top of Window to Floor _____

Type of Covering (draperies, blinds, etc.) _____

Purchased From _____ Cost $_____ Date _____

    Measurements of Window Covering _____

    Fabric & Cleaning Instructions _____

Cleaned By _____ Cost $_____ Date _____

WALL COVERING

Wall Measurements

North _____ South _____ East _____ West _____

Note: Use "2nd Type of Covering" for woodwork or panelling. It has a "Refinished By" section.

1st Type of Covering (paint, paper, etc.) _____

Purchased From _____ Date _____

    Brand & Pattern _____

    Color & No. _____ Warranty Period _____

    Cost/Unit $_____ No. of Units _____ Total $_____

Installed By _____

    Date _____ Cost $_____

Notes: _____

2nd Type of Covering (woodwork, panelling, etc.) _____

Purchased From _____ Date _____

    Brand & Pattern _____

    Color & No. _____ Warranty Period _____

    Cost/Unit $_____ No. of Units _____ Total $_____

Installed By _____

    Date _____ Cost $_____

Refinished By _____

    Date _____ Cost $_____

Notes: _____

SAMPLES: PAINT, WALLPAPER, ETC.

attach swatch or paint daub here

FURNITURE/APPLIANCES

Item	Purchased From	Date	Cost	Warranty

EXTRA NOTES

(Use tick marks at top & bottom to make graph paper)

MISCELLANEOUS ROOM 2

FLOOR COVERING

Floor Measurements

Widest part of room from middle of doorway _____

Longest part of room from middle of doorway _____

Notes: _____

Type of Covering (carpet, hardwood, etc.) _____

Purchased From _____ Date _____

Brand & Pattern _____

Color & No. _____ Warranty Period _____

Type of Backing _____ Pad Type _____

Cost/Unit $_____ No. of Units _____ Total $_____

Installed By _____ Attached With _____

Date _____ Cost $_____

Cleaned/Refinished By _____

Date 1 _____ Cost $_____

Date 2 _____ Cost $_____

Notes: _____

_____

CEILING COVERING

Type of Covering (paint, spray texture, etc.) _____

Purchased From _____ Date _____

Brand & Pattern _____

Color & No. _____ Warranty Period _____

Applied with (texture roller, sprayer, etc.) _____

Cost/Unit $_____ No. of Units _____ Total $_____

Installed By _____

Date _____ Cost $_____

Notes: _____

_____

WINDOW COVERING

Window 1 Measurements

Height _____ Width _____ Top of Window to Floor _____

Type of Covering (draperies, blinds, etc.) _____

Purchased From _____ Cost $_____ Date _____

    Measurements of Window Covering _____

    Fabric & Cleaning Instructions _____

Cleaned By _____ Cost $_____ Date _____

Notes: _____

_____

Window 2 Measurements

Height _____ Width _____ Top of Window to Floor _____

Type of Covering (draperies, blinds, etc.) _____

Purchased From _____ Cost $_____ Date _____

    Measurements of Window Covering _____

    Fabric & Cleaning Instructions _____

Cleaned By _____ Cost $_____ Date _____

Notes: _____

_____

Window 3 Measurements

Height _____ Width _____ Top of Window to Floor _____

Type of Covering (draperies, blinds, etc.) _____

Purchased From _____ Cost $_____ Date _____

    Measurements of Window Covering _____

    Fabric & Cleaning Instructions _____

Cleaned By _____ Cost $_____ Date _____

Notes: _____

_____

Window 4 Measurements

Height _____ Width _____ Top of Window to Floor _____

Type of Covering (draperies, blinds, etc.) _____

Purchased From _____ Cost $_____ Date _____

    Measurements of Window Covering _____

    Fabric & Cleaning Instructions _____

Cleaned By _____ Cost $_____ Date _____

WALL COVERING

Wall Measurements

North _____ South _____ East _____ West _____

Note: Use "2nd Type of Covering" for woodwork or panelling. It has a "Refinished By" section.

1st Type of Covering (paint, paper, etc.) _____

Purchased From _____ Date _____

    Brand & Pattern _____

    Color & No. _____ Warranty Period _____

    Cost/Unit $_____ No. of Units _____ Total $_____

Installed By _____

    Date _____ Cost $_____

Notes: _____

2nd Type of Covering (woodwork, panelling, etc.) _____

Purchased From _____ Date _____

    Brand & Pattern _____

    Color & No. _____ Warranty Period _____

    Cost/Unit $_____ No. of Units _____ Total $_____

Installed By _____

    Date _____ Cost $_____

Refinished By _____

    Date _____ Cost $_____

Notes: _____

SAMPLES: PAINT, WALLPAPER, ETC.

attach swatch or paint daub here

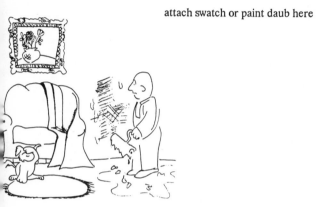

FURNITURE/APPLIANCES

Item	Purchased From	Date	Cost	Warranty

<u>EXTRA NOTES</u>

(Use tick marks at top & bottom to make graph paper)

MISCELLANEOUS ROOM 3
FLOOR COVERING

Floor Measurements

Widest part of room from middle of doorway _____

Longest part of room from middle of doorway _____

Notes: _____

Type of Covering (carpet, hardwood, etc.) _____

Purchased From _____ Date _____

Brand & Pattern _____

Color & No. _____ Warranty Period _____

Type of Backing _____ Pad Type _____

Cost/Unit $_____ No. of Units _____ Total $_____

Installed By _____ Attached With _____

Date _____ Cost $_____

Cleaned/Refinished By _____

Date 1 _____ Cost $_____

Date 2 _____ Cost $_____

Notes: _____

_____

CEILING COVERING

Type of Covering (paint, spray texture, etc.) _____

Purchased From _____ Date _____

Brand & Pattern _____

Color & No. _____ Warranty Period _____

Applied with (texture roller, sprayer, etc.) _____

Cost/Unit $_____ No. of Units _____ Total $_____

Installed By _____

Date _____ Cost $_____

Notes: _____

_____

WINDOW COVERING

Window 1 Measurements

Height _____ Width _____ Top of Window to Floor _____

Type of Covering (draperies, blinds, etc.) _____

Purchased From _____ Cost $_____ Date _____

   Measurements of Window Covering _____

   Fabric & Cleaning Instructions _____

Cleaned By _____ Cost $_____ Date _____

Notes: _____

_____

Window 2 Measurements

Height _____ Width _____ Top of Window to Floor _____

Type of Covering (draperies, blinds, etc.) _____

Purchased From _____ Cost $_____ Date _____

   Measurements of Window Covering _____

   Fabric & Cleaning Instructions _____

Cleaned By _____ Cost $_____ Date _____

Notes: _____

_____

Window 3 Measurements

Height _____ Width _____ Top of Window to Floor _____

Type of Covering (draperies, blinds, etc.) _____

Purchased From _____ Cost $_____ Date _____

   Measurements of Window Covering _____

   Fabric & Cleaning Instructions _____

Cleaned By _____ Cost $_____ Date _____

Notes: _____

_____

Window 4 Measurements

Height _____ Width _____ Top of Window to Floor _____

Type of Covering (draperies, blinds, etc.) _____

Purchased From _____ Cost $_____ Date _____

   Measurements of Window Covering _____

   Fabric & Cleaning Instructions _____

Cleaned By _____ Cost $_____ Date _____

WALL COVERING

Wall Measurements

North _____ South _____ East _____ West _____

Note: Use "2nd Type of Covering" for woodwork or panelling. It has a "Refinished By" section.

1st Type of Covering (paint, paper, etc.) _____

Purchased From _____ Date _____

   Brand & Pattern _____

   Color & No. _____ Warranty Period _____

   Cost/Unit $_____ No. of Units _____ Total $_____

Installed By _____

   Date _____ Cost $_____

Notes: _____

2nd Type of Covering (woodwork, panelling, etc.) _____

Purchased From _____ Date _____

   Brand & Pattern _____

   Color & No. _____ Warranty Period _____

   Cost/Unit $_____ No. of Units _____ Total $_____

Installed By _____

   Date _____ Cost $_____

Refinished By _____

   Date _____ Cost $_____

Notes: _____

SAMPLES: PAINT, WALLPAPER, ETC.

attach swatch or paint daub here

FURNITURE/APPLIANCES

Item	Purchased From	Date	Cost	Warranty

EXTRA NOTES

STORAGE/CLOSETS

DECK

Type of Wood (redwood, pine, etc.) _____

Purchased From _____ Date _____

   Sealed/Finished With _____

   Brand, Color & No. _____

Installed By _____ Total Cost $_____

Note: In general, solid color oil or latex stains are not recommended for use on floors, porches, decks, or similar areas that may be walked upon.

Refinished With _____

   Date _____ Cost $_____

Notes: _____

_____

_____

_____

_____

DRIVEWAY

Type of Driveway (asphalt, concrete, etc.) _____

Sealed With (brand, type, & no.) _____

   Purchased From _____ Date _____

   Cost/Unit $_____ No. of Units _____ Total $_____

Sealed With (brand, type, & no.) _____

   Purchased From _____ Date _____

   Cost/Unit $_____ No. of Units _____ Total $_____

Sealed With (brand, type, & no.) _____

   Purchased From _____ Date _____

   Cost/Unit $_____ No. of Units _____ Total $_____

Notes: _____

_____

_____

_____

FENCE

Type of Wood (redwood, pine, etc.) _____

Purchased From _____ Date _____

   Sealed/Finished With _____

   Brand, Color & No. _____ Latex ____ Oil ____

Installed By _____ Total Cost $_____

Refinished With _____

   Date _____ Cost $_____

Notes: _____

_____

PATIO

Type of Material (patio blocks, cement, etc.) _____

Sealed/Finished With _____

Installed By _____ Date _____

Total Cost $_____

Notes: _____

_____

PORCH

(Use tick marks at top & bottom to make graph paper)

GARAGE
FLOOR

Type of Floor (asphalt, concrete, etc.) _____

Sealed/Finished With (brand, color, & no.) _____

    Purchased From _____ Date _____

    Cost/Unit $_____ No. of Units _____ Total $_____

Notes: _____

_____

_____

GUTTERS & DOWNSPOUTS

Type of Material (steel, aluminum, etc.) _____

Purchased From _____ Date _____

    Cost $_____ Warranty Period _____

Installed By _____ Date _____

Notes: _____

_____

ROOF

Type of Roofing (fiberglass shingles, cedar shakes, etc.) _____

Purchased From _____

    Brand, Color, & No. _____

    Cost/Unit $_____ No. of Units _____ Total $_____

    Misc. Materials _____ Cost $_____

Installed By _____ Cost $_____

    Date _____ Warranty Period _____

Total Materials Cost $ _____ Entire Job Cost $_____

Maintenance (preservative or sealer) _____

_____

Notes: _____

_____

_____

SIDING

__1st Type of Siding__ (brick, stucco, etc.) _____

Purchased From _____ Date _____ Cost $_____

   Brand, Color, & No. _____ Warranty Period _____

Type of Finish (paint, stain, etc.) _____

   Purchased From _____ Date _____

   Brand, Color, & No. _____ Warranty Period _____

   Cost/Unit $_____ No. of Units _____ Total $_____

Installed By _____

   Date _____ Cost $_____

Notes: _____

_____

_____

_____

_____

__2nd Type of Siding__ (brick, stucco, etc.) _____

Purchased From _____ Date _____ Cost $_____

   Brand, Color, & No. _____ Warranty Period _____

Type of Finish (paint, stain, etc.) _____

   Purchased From _____ Date _____

   Brand, Color, & No. _____ Warranty Period _____

   Cost/Unit $_____ No. of Units _____ Total $_____

Installed By _____

   Date _____ Cost $_____

Notes: _____

_____

_____

_____

_____

TRIM

<u>1st Type of Trim</u> (wood, aluminum, etc.) _____

Purchased From _____ Date _____ Cost $_____

    Brand, Color, & No. _____ Warranty Period _____

Type of Finish (paint, stain, etc.) _____

    Purchased From _____ Date _____

    Brand, Color, & No. _____ Warranty Period _____

    Cost/Unit $_____ No. of Units _____ Total $_____

Installed By _____

    Date _____ Cost $_____

Notes: _____

_____

<u>2nd Type of Trim</u> (wood, aluminum, etc.) _____

Purchased From _____ Date _____ Cost $_____

    Brand, Color, & No. _____ Warranty Period _____

Type of Finish (paint, stain, etc.) _____

    Purchased From _____ Date _____

    Brand, Color, & No. _____ Warranty Period _____

    Cost/Unit $_____ No. of Units _____ Total $_____

Installed By _____

    Date _____ Cost $_____

Notes: _____

WALLS & CEILING

<u>Type of Material</u> (gypsum board, etc.) _____

    Purchased From _____ Date _____

    Cost/Unit $_____ No. of Units _____ Total $_____

    Sealed/Finished With (brand, color, & no.) _____

Notes: _____

_____

HOUSE EXTERIOR
GUTTERS & DOWNSPOUTS

Type of Material (steel, aluminum, etc.) _____

Purchased From _____ Date _____

    Cost $_____ Warranty Period _____

Installed By _____ Date _____

Notes: _____

_____

_____

_____

_____

_____

_____

ROOF

Type of Roofing (fiberglass shingles, cedar shakes, etc.) _____

Purchased From _____

    Brand, Color, & No. _____

    Cost/Unit $_____ No. of Units _____ Total $_____

    Misc. Materials _____ Cost $_____

Installed By _____ Cost $_____

    Date _____ Warranty Period _____

Total Materials Cost $ _____ Entire Job Cost $_____

Maintenance (preservative or sealer) _____

_____

Notes: _____

_____

STORM DOORS

_____

_____

_____

111

SIDING

1st Type of Siding (brick, stucco, etc.) _____

Purchased From _____ Date _____ Cost $_____

   Brand, Color, & No. _____ Warranty Period _____

Type of Finish (paint, stain, etc.) _____

    Purchased From _____ Date _____

    Brand, Color, & No. _____ Warranty Period _____

    Cost/Unit $_____ No. of Units _____ Total $_____

Installed By _____

    Date _____ Cost $_____

Notes: _____

_____

2nd Type of Siding (brick, stucco, etc.) _____

Purchased From _____ Date _____ Cost $_____

   Brand, Color, & No. _____ Warranty Period _____

Type of Finish (paint, stain, etc.) _____

    Purchased From _____ Date _____

    Brand, Color, & No. _____ Warranty Period _____

    Cost/Unit $_____ No. of Units _____ Total $_____

Installed By _____

    Date _____ Cost $_____

Notes: _____

STORM WINDOWS

Type of Frame (wood, aluminum, etc.) _____

Use "Trim" on page 113 for "Type of Finish"

Purchased From _____ Date _____

   Cost $_____ Warranty Period _____

Installed By _____ Cost $_____

Notes: _____

<u>TRIM</u>

<u>1st Type of Trim</u> (wood, aluminum, etc.) _____

Purchased From _____ Date _____ Cost $_____

    Brand, Color, & No. _____ Warranty Period _____

Type of Finish (paint, stain, etc.) _____

    Purchased From _____ Date _____

    Brand, Color, & No. _____ Warranty Period _____

    Cost/Unit $_____ No. of Units _____ Total $_____

Installed By _____

    Date _____ Cost $_____

Notes: _____

_____

_____

<u>2nd Type of Trim</u> (wood, aluminum, etc.) _____

Purchased From _____ Date _____ Cost $_____

    Brand, Color, & No. _____ Warranty Period _____

Type of Finish (paint, stain, etc.) _____

    Purchased From _____ Date _____

    Brand, Color, & No. _____ Warranty Period _____

    Cost/Unit $_____ No. of Units _____ Total $_____

Installed By _____

    Date _____ Cost $_____

Notes: _____

_____

<u>EXTRA NOTES</u>

_____

_____

_____

COOLING & HEATING
AIR CONDITIONER

Type of Unit (electric, natural gas, etc.) _____

Manufacturer & Model_____ Efficiency _____

Purchased From _____ Date _____

    Cost $_____ Warranty Period _____

    Filter Type _____ Size _____

Cleaned/Serviced By _____

    Date No. 1 _____ Cost $_____

    Date No. 2 _____ Cost $_____

Notes: _____

_____

_____

_____

FIREPLACE

Insert Mfr. & Model_____

Purchased From _____ Date _____

    Cost $_____ Warranty Period _____

Installed By _____ Cost $_____ Date _____

Chimney Cleaned By _____

    Date _____ Cost $_____

Notes: _____

_____

_____

_____

HEAT EXCHANGER

_____

_____

_____

_____

_____

HEAT PUMP

Type of Unit (electric, fuel oil, etc.) _____

Manufacturer & Model_____ Efficiency _____

Purchased From _____ Date _____

    Cost $_____ Warranty Period _____

    Filter Type _____ Size _____

Cleaned/Serviced By _____

    Date _____ Cost $_____

Notes: _____

_____

HEATING PLANT (Furnace)

Type of Unit (electric, fuel oil, etc.) _____

Manufacturer & Model_____ Efficiency _____

Purchased From _____ Date _____

    Cost $_____ Warranty Period _____

    Filter Type _____ Size _____

    Humidifier _____

Cleaned/Serviced By _____

    Date No. 1 _____ Cost $_____

    Date No. 2 _____ Cost $_____

Notes: _____

_____

WOOD STOVE

Manufacturer & Model_____ Efficiency _____

Purchased From _____ Date _____

    Cost $_____ Warranty Period _____

Chimney Cleaned By _____

    Date _____ Cost $ _____

Notes: _____

_____

INSULATION

ATTIC

Type of Insulation (fiberglass rolls, etc.) _____ Cost $_____

    Thickness _____ R-Value Added _____

    Previous R-Value _____ Aggregate R-Value _____

    Type of Vapor Barrier (6 mill poly, etc.) _____

Installed By _____ Date _____

Total Material Cost $_____ Labor Cost $_____ Total Cost $_____

Notes: _____

_____

_____

Type of Venting Note: You should have one sq. ft. of free-flowing cross-ventilation for every 150 sq. ft. of attic floor space. Soffit vents with screen covers can reduce air flow by up to 75%.

Under Eave (Soffit) Sq. Inches ____ Louvered Attic Vents Sq. Inches _____

Low Pitch Slant Roof Vents Sq. Inches_____ Turbines Sq. Inches _____

Other _____

Notes: _____

_____

_____

WALLS

1st Type of Insulation (fiberglass, etc.) _____

    Thickness _____ R-Value _____ Cost $_____

2nd Type of Insulation (extruded polystyrene, etc.) _____

    Thickness _____ R-Value _____ Cost $_____

Aggregate R-Value _____ Warranty Period _____

Type of Vapor Barrier (6 mill poly, etc.) _____

Installed By _____ Date _____

Total Material Cost $_____ Labor Cost $_____ Total Cost $_____

Notes: _____

_____

OTHER INSULATION (rim joist, exterior foundation, etc.)

DOOR CHIMES

_____

_____

_____

_____

GARAGE DOOR OPENER

_____

_____

_____

_____

_____

INTERCOM SYSTEM

_____

_____

_____

_____

SECURITY SYSTEM

_____

_____

_____

_____

_____

SMOKE/FIRE DETECTORS

_____

_____

_____

_____

TELEPHONES/ANSWERING MACHINE

THERMOSTAT

RADON TESTING & INFORMATION

SEWER/CESSPOOL/SEPTIC TANK

SUMP PUMP

_____
_____
_____

_____

SWIMMING POOL

_____
_____
_____
_____
_____
_____
_____
_____
_____
_____
_____
_____
_____
_____
_____
_____
_____
_____
_____
_____
_____
_____

WATER HEATER

_____
_____
_____
_____

WATER SOFTENER

_____
_____
_____
_____

WELL

_____
_____
_____
_____
_____

WHIRLPOOL/HOT TUB/SAUNA

_____
_____
_____
_____
_____

WHOLE HOUSE VACUUM

_____
_____
_____
_____
_____

EXTRA NOTES

(Use tick marks at top & bottom to make graph paper)

EXTRA NOTES

(Use tick marks at top & bottom to make graph paper)

EXTRA NOTES

(Use tick marks at top & bottom to make graph paper)

EXTRA NOTES

(Use tick marks at top & bottom to make graph paper)

ANNUAL INCOME AND CAPITAL GAIN TAXES

NOTICE: *The following is a general overview of some of the important concepts to consider when accumulating the information you will need in the future to determine annual income or capital gain tax on the sale of your principal residence. It is not intended to be a complete discussion of all the tax implications of these types of costs. If you have any questions, seek the advice of a qualified tax professional.*

Your principal residence (home) is usually the most significant asset you acquire. Proper recordkeeping is essential to avoid paying unnecessary income tax when you sell your home. In addition to the original acquisition costs of your home, many of your closing, decorating, maintenance, and remodeling costs can reduce your annual income taxes and capital gain taxes.

In general, the tax basis for your principal residence initially means the total amount you paid that can be attributed to the purchase or construction of your home. This usually means the amount of cash paid, whether it is a down-payment or any indebtedness the property is subject to at the time of purchase.

Additionally, any out-of-pocket costs for commissions or other purchasing expenses incurred when acquiring your home should be included in the total acquisition cost of your home. These out-of-pocket costs include such items as attorney, escrow, or appraisal fees, title cost, and loan placement charges, unless you deducted those fees as interest deductions in the year you bought your home.

Subsequent amounts you pay for additions to your home such as: storm windows; room additions; finishing the attic, basement, or other room; new plumbing, heating system, or furnace; installing an air conditioning system; adding a new roof; and land improvements like swimming pools and landscaping are all additional costs which need to be documented and added to the original cost basis of your home.

When you sell your home, income tax rules require that you produce sufficient documentation to verify the original cost basis of your home and any subsequent additions to that cost basis. Therefore, you must permanently retain supporting documents, e.g. closing documents; contractor invoices for improvements; and paid invoices for improvements, remodeling, or renovation work. Make sure your invoices show the type of work done and the date completed. Write the information on the invoice if it is not there. (See the "How To File Important Papers" chapter for a simple, easy-to-use filing system).

On pages 128-129 there is an easy-to-complete tax worksheet. This worksheet will make it easy to maintain an ongoing summary of essential cost information you need to keep. Make it a routine to enter your improvements, remodeling, and renovation expenditures starting with the date you purchased your home. Include all costs associated with the purchase. If you are diligent in updating the tax worksheet, it will be a handy reference for determining, for tax purposes, the cumulative amount you have invested in your home at any given point. Remember, you must still keep all receipts and invoices for proof.

It is important that you understand the difference between "repairs" and "improvements." Repairs are generally considered to be those types of expenditures which merely keep the principal residence in its ordinary operating condition and do not materially add to its value or prolong its useful life. Typical examples of repair items include repainting; replacing broken windows; and repairing and fixing gutters, floors, driveways, and electrical or plumbing fixtures. These items are not currently deductible for income tax purposes and are not considered additions to the tax basis of your principal residence. While, there is no *tax* reason to accumulate these costs, they are quite useful for home planning and budgeting.

There are always exceptions to the rule. For example, an item normally considered to be a "repair" can be considered an "improvement" if it is done as part of a mass remodeling or renovation project.

Improvements are generally defined as those items which add to the value, prolong the life, or make some modification to the use of the principal residence. Some examples are adding new plumbing or wiring, a new roof, paving the driveway, landscaping, or putting on an addition.

Improvements are considered additions to your initial investment in your principal residence. Improvement costs, including materials and labor charges, should be added to the tax worksheet and treated as additional expenditures. However, you cannot add the cost of your own hard labor to the project.

Even though you elect to finance the improvements over a period of time, your total investment in your home is increased immediately to reflect the full cost of the improvements. Furthermore, if you finance the improvements by taking out a second mortgage or other form of financing obligation, those additional costs (appraisal fees, title fees, or legal expenses) are considered part of the total improvement.

Special thanks for this valuable tax information goes to Thomas A. Dougherty. Mr. Dougherty is a certified public accountant and licensed attorney. He provides corporate and individual tax consulting services to emerging and established privately-owned businesses.

TAX WORKSHEET

	Amount
Original Cost of Home Per Purchase Agreement	_____
Add:	

Closing Costs:

	Amount
Legal Fees	_____
Appraisal Fee	_____
Commission Fee to Broker	_____
Escrow Fee	_____
Title Cost	_____
State Deed Taxes and Filing Fees	_____
Loan Placement Fees (e.g. Points)	_____

Remodeling and Renovations Made:

Date	Description	Amount

Improvements Made:

Date	Description	Amount

HOW TO FILE IMPORTANT PAPERS

Every home owner needs to keep important documents and receipts for tax, insurance, warranty, or budget purposes. These papers can easily be misplaced if you don't have a system to manage them. However, a filing system that is too complex is as bad as none at all because you won't take the time to use it.

Starting a home filing system should save you a great deal of money, time, and aggravation and will reduce your likelihood of hearing these two dreadful statements:

"Your warranty is void without the original receipt" or "We cannot accept your tax deduction without the proper documentation."

After considerable research and experimentation, I developed a filing system that is easy to use, easy on my time, flexible, and inexpensive to start. All it consists of is:

1. Two large expanding folders with individual pockets and preprinted alphabetic tabs: (1) one set is for filing papers dealing with the *purchase of your home* and any *work done on your home* and (2) the other set is to file receipts for things you *buy for your home and family*. Two file systems eliminate what could be a huge sorting problem when tax information must be separated from ordinary purchases.

2. A household inventory for insurance purposes.

The supplies for this system are inexpensive, especially when compared to the money, time, and patience you may lose without them. They are available in many book, stationery, and variety stores.

Label one file set "Home Owner's Journal." This set is for filing papers dealing with the *purchase of your home* and any *work done on your home*. Keep only photocopies of important receipts in this file (put the originals in your safe-deposit box). Include receipts for budgeting, planning, and tax purposes (see Annual Income and Capital Gain Tax chapter). This file should also contain copies of purchase agreements and other closing documents from the purchase your home, receipts for repairs, additions, installation, purchases, care or cleaning instructions, and contractor business cards, etc.

File each item under the appropriate letter in the alphabet. For example, living room carpet receipts, warranties, care instructions, the installer's business card, etc. should be stapled together, labeled "living room carpet", and filed under "C" for carpet. Don't forget to make appropriate notes on the documents such as "date purchased," if they are not already marked.

If you are not sure where to file something, put it in the most obvious place and put a "See _____" cross-reference note where it could also be filed. Periodically purge the file of information you no longer need, such as expired warranties and receipts for old paint you wallpapered over.

The second file set should be labeled "Purchases." This set is for all the receipts, care and cleaning instructions, warranty cards, serial numbers, and instruction booklets for things you *buy for your home and family* such as appliances, electronics, furniture, wrist watches, etc. File each of these items under the appropriate letter of the alphabet. Follow the same filing instructions as in the previous paragraphs.

It is a good idea to maintain a written inventory of the contents of your home for insurance purposes in case of fire or burglary. A written inventory is perhaps easiest done with a good home inventory journal like those available in book, stationery, and variety stores. Look for one that allows you some flexibility. Many books are so specific that much of the book is wasted with items that don't apply to you. Some can also leave you short of room for the things you do have. If you are very thorough, a tablet will also work.

Photographs or a video tape are good complements too, but not substitutes for the written inventory. They help show the condition of the item, which is important if you have an "actual cash value" insurance policy (which is often based on the depreciated value) instead of the "replacement value." Ask your insurance agent which type you have. The difference in your premium may not be that much and replacement cost is often well worth the difference.

Another alternative to paper is a tape recorder. As with video tape, however, updates are difficult to make unless added to the end of the tape.

Whichever method you choose, make sure it fits into your safe-deposit box. That is where you should keep it once it is complete. Update it whenever necessary, but return it when finished. Keep a copy at home for reference.

For more information on how to have an efficient household and painlessly deal with the tons of paperwork, see pages 132-133. One excellent book is *File...Don't Pile*™, by Pat Dorff. Her system is remarkable for efficiently taking care of the worst paperwork problems. Another is Bonnie McCullough's *Totally Organized*. This easy reading book shows you how to organize anything, including your thoughts, time, and kids. Both books are unique and are valuable reading. The *Weekly Menu Planner and Shopping List* is terrific for making a dreadful weekly activity quite easy. Finally, if you want to gain control of your personal and family finances, try *Common Cent$*.

THE "GET ORGANIZED" BOOKSHELF

The Home Owner's Journal: What I Did & When I Did It, by Colleen Jenkins. Are you playing Hide and Seek with your home decorating and repair records? Here's the answer to every homeowner's dream. The Home Owner's Journal lets you keep all your important home details at your fingertips! You'll know how much paint it took to do the kitchen the last time and when something was last cleaned, serviced, or repaired. Simply fill in the blanks as it guides you step by step. Save yourself money, time, and frustration by recording everything in ONE place. Delightfully illustrated, fill-in-the-blank book. A great gift for housewarmings, weddings, Christmas, and birthdays. Softcover, 136 pages, 6" x 9", spiral binding, $9.95*

The Family Memory Book: Highlights of Our Times Together, by Judy Lawrence helps you keep precious memories *forever*! The specially designed, fill-in-the-blank format captures and preserves, for lifelong enjoyment, 5 full years of keepsake personal memories by helping you to effortlessly record the highlights of holidays, special events and other occasions. The simple, step-by-step process motivates even readers who have long wanted to record these special events, but haven't known how or where to start. Hardcover, 96 pages, 7" x 10", $14.95*

The Weekly Menu Planner & Shopping List. In one easy step, busy cooks can plan a week's worth of meals and have an organized shopping list ready for a *fast* trip to the market -- all on one sheet. The top "Menu" portion is in calendar format and shows your family "what's cooking" that week; the bottom "Shopping List" portion helps you and your family prepare your list for those meals quickly! Includes a full year's supply -- 52 sheets -- one for each week. It helps you get organized, shop faster, save grocery money, keep the right foods in stock, and eat healthier. A great gift for families *on the go*. Charming country design. FREE BONUS! We'll enclose the brochure Eating for a Healthy Heart and to Help Prevent Cancer. 8 1/2" x 11", $6.95*

File...Don't Pile!™, by Pat Dorff. This book is for anyone who has ever watched the stacks of papers, magazines, and clippings pile up out of control. More than a collection of random hints, this handy guide provides systems for organizing every conceivable type of household paper. If you want fast, easy, practical advice on what papers to save, where to store it, when to throw away, and how to remember where you filed it, then this is it! Full of how-to diagrams. Softcover, 224 pages, 5 1/2" x 8 1/4", $8.95*

Totally Organized The Bonnie McCullough Way, by Bonnie McCullough. If you need help organizing your time, your thoughts, your budget, even your kids, then this is the book for you. Learn how to keep a planning notebook, prepare effective lists, set priorities and goals, start and keep a budget, and cut your food and clothing costs by smart planning. Bonnie offers tips on housework and explains how to work smarter not harder. Full of how-to diagrams. Softcover, 299 pages, 5 1/2" x 8 1/4", $11.95*

Common Cent\$: The Complete Money Management Workbook, by money counselor Judy Lawrence. No matter what your income level or profession, this easy-to-use book will help you gain control of your finances by showing you where your money is going -- and where it SHOULD be going. Learn to manage your income properly and plan ahead for monthly and yearly obligations. It's filled with money-saving tips, monthly and yearly budget worksheets, and expense records. Softcover, 84 pages, spiral binding, 11" x 8 1/4", $10.95[*]

401 Ways To Get Your Kids To Work At Home, by Bonnie McCullough & Susan Monson. These tips are household tested and proven effective! This book provides techniques, tips, tricks, and strategies on how to get your kids to share in the housework and become self-reliant, responsible adults. Whether your kids are toddlers or teenagers, you'll find immediate help and direction. Learn how and when to assign and teach specific jobs (starting from age 2); how to give positive feedback, incentives, and rewards (or punishment); and how to teach your child to organize his or her bedroom, handle personal hygiene and clothing needs, cooking, nutrition, shopping skills, and more. Softcover, 245 pages, 5 1/2" x 8 1/4", $8.95[*]

With Love From My Kitchen, by Nancy Radcliffe Edwards. Do you wish you had a copy of your grandmother's favorite recipes? Ever dream of writing your own personal family cookbook? Your children would love it! This write-your-own cookbook is beautifully illustrated with a charming collection of quaint, old-fashioned drawings on lined recipe pages. Hardcover, 264 pages, 6 1/4" x 8 1/2", spiral binding, 12 pre-printed mylar protected tab dividers, easy-to-do indexes, and a special section for secrets and hints. $18.95[*]

[*]**Prices effective 1/92 and are subject to change.**

Turn Page For Order Form

Blue Sky Marketing, Inc.
P.O. Box 21583-S, St. Paul, MN, 55121-1583, USA
(612) 456-5602.

ORDER FORM

COMPLETE SATISFACTION GUARANTEED
(100% refund if you're not)

Qty.   **YES! Please send me:**

_____ The Home Owner's Journal $9.95* each

_____ Weekly Menu Plan. & Shopping List $6.95* each

_____ File...Don't Pile!TM $8.95* each

_____ Totally Organized $10.95* each

_____ The Family Memory Book $14.95* each

_____ Common Cent$ $10.95* each

_____ 401 Ways t/g Your Kids To Work At Home $8.95* each

_____ With Love From My Kitchen $18.95* each

Shipping to U.S.A. addresses (to ship UPS we must have your <u>STREET</u> address)
* 1 book, add $2.50 for U.S. Mail "book rate" (may take 4 weeks) or $3.50 for UPS.
* 2-4 books, UPS (or 1st Class Mail) for *only* $3.50!
* 5+ books, FREE shipping!!!
* Call or write for shipping charges to addresses outside the U.S.A.

Total for Merchandise* _____
MN residents add 6.5% tax _____
Shipping Charges (see above for rates) _____
TOTAL _____

U.S. currency please, if ordering from outside the U.S.A.
Check or credit card only. Please Print!

__Payment enclosed __Please charge my: __Visa __Mastercard __Discover

Card #_____ Exp. Date _____

Signature _____

Name (please print) _____

Address _____

City, State, ZIP _____

Daytime Phone (for questions about your order)_____

SEND TO:
Blue Sky Marketing Inc, PO Box 21583-S, St. Paul, MN 55121-1583 USA
or **CALL TOLL FREE: 1-800-444-5450** or **(612)456-5602** in Mpls/St Paul

*Prices effective 1/92 and are subject to change.

Turn Page for Additional Order Form

ORDER FORM

COMPLETE SATISFACTION GUARANTEED
(100% refund if you're not)

Qty.   **YES! Please send me:**

_____ The Home Owner's Journal $9.95* each

_____ Weekly Menu Plan. & Shopping List $6.95* each

_____ File...Don't Pile!™ $8.95* each

_____ Totally Organized $10.95* each

_____ The Family Memory Book $14.95* each

_____ Common Cent$ $10.95* each

_____ 401 Ways t/g Your Kids To Work At Home $8.95* each

_____ With Love From My Kitchen $18.95* each

Shipping to U.S.A. addresses (to ship UPS we must have your <u>STREET</u> address)
* 1 book, add $2.50 for U.S. Mail "book rate" (may take 4 weeks) or $3.50 for UPS.
* 2-4 books, UPS (or 1st Class Mail) for *only* $3.50!
* 5+ books, FREE shipping!!!
* Call or write for shipping charges to addresses outside the U.S.A.

<u>Total for Merchandise</u>*_____
<u>MN residents add 6.5% tax</u>_____
<u>Shipping Charges (see above for rates)</u>_____
TOTAL_____

U.S. currency please, if ordering from outside the U.S.A.
Check or credit card only. Please Print!

__Payment enclosed   __Please charge my: __Visa   __Mastercard   __Discover

Card #_____ Exp. Date _____

Signature _____

Name (please print) _____

Address _____

City, State, ZIP _____

Daytime Phone (for questions about your order)_____

SEND TO:
Blue Sky Marketing Inc, PO Box 21583-S, St. Paul, MN 55121-1583 USA
or **CALL TOLL FREE: 1-800-444-5450** or **(612)456-5602** in Mpls/St Paul

*Prices effective 1/92 and are subject to change.